Peninnis Lighthouse.

INTRODUCTION: ST MARY'S

When you first arrive on the quay at Hugh Town, it's a surprise to find that you've stepped into a whirlpool of noise and confusion: shouting as suitcases are relocated and passed overhead, as boxes of flowers and crates of live crabs and lobsters (some making a break for freedom across the quay) are loaded for the mainland. Where is the tranquillity you imagined when you leafed through the pictures of remote beaches in the tourist brochure?

In fact, of course, this organised chaos of criss-crossing arrivals, transfers and departures is very much a part of island life; a mini version is performed every day on the tiny off-island quays too. But like the tide which does so much to govern life on Scilly, the melee soon ebbs as changeovers are made, passengers are dispatched and with three blasts of its horn, the *Scillonian* departs for the mainland. Then, all of a sudden the noise and the hubbub on the quay is gone and you're left with the smell of the sea, the cries of the gulls and that beautiful Scillonian landscape – sea, sandbank and granite carn – that you travelled all this way to see.

St Mary's is the largest of Scilly's five inhabited islands and home to three-quarters of Scilly's 2,200 residents who mostly live in Hugh Town and Old Town. It acts as a stepping stone to the more remote and rugged off-islands and, unlike them, retains a little of the character of the mainland. It has proper tarmac roads and, although you cannot bring your own car here, you can book a taxi that will drop you off at the other end of the island. You can then saunter back at your own pace along the coast path calling in at cafes on the way. Electric carts and bicycles are also available to hire.

If you're staying in Hugh Town there are three popular walks that start from here that will help you get your bearings: one circles the Garrison, another follows the coast south from Porthcressa to Peninnis Head and the third heads north along the coast to Porthloo. The rest of St Mary's coast can be split into easy sections: Old Town to Porth Hellick, Porth Hellick to Watermill Cove and Watermill Cove to Bar Point and Porthloo. At any one of these places you can turn inland to make your own circular walks using the country lanes and nature trails at Lower and Higher Moors to cross the island. Each walk takes a morning or an afternoon to complete and so a pair of walks can be put together based around lunch at one of the cafes on the north of St Mary's.

This book follows the coast in a roughly anti-clockwise direction from Hugh Town. Many visitors will understandably spend the bulk of their time exploring St Mary's coast, but the centre of the island rewards exploration too. The small mixed farms here supply the needs of the islands and there are also fields of flowers that are sent to the mainland in the winter months. Holy Vale is a particularly beautiful spot and you can tour the vineyard here and taste the local Pinot Noir at the winery (check opening times before you go). As you walk the island you'll also come across various studios, potteries and galleries along the way.

St Mary's has many impressive prehistoric monuments and, if you're interested in the ancient history of the islands, it's a good plan to spend a bit of time visiting places like the Giant's Tomb on Porth Hellick Down, Innisidgen Tomb and Bant's Carn Tomb at Halangy Down where you can also wander around the remains of 2,000-year-old houses. These prehistoric monuments are kept clear of bracken and brambles and have information boards so that when you get to the off-islands – whose ancient sites are often a little tumbled down and overgrown – you already have a clear picture in your own mind of what you're looking for among the vegetation and rocks.

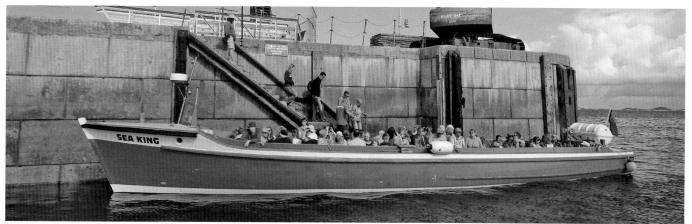

Off-island ferries and sightseeing boats leave from Hugh Town Quay.

For nature lovers, there are lots of wildlife boat trips from the quay at Hugh Town, including one on a glass-bottomed boat, as well as lectures and slide shows in the Church Hall. Boat trips to see the puffins, seals and shearwaters on the more remote isles are particularly popular. Porth Hellick Pool is a favourite spot in the spring and autumn for migrating birds who stop here to rest and refuel. Sometimes when gales blow in exotic birds from North America, hundreds of birdwatchers will descend on the islands. They can be found crouching in hedgerows and craning their necks over walls to catch sight of unusual visitors.

It's perfectly possible to walk all the way around the coast of St Mary's in a single day. It's about 12.9km or 8 miles (not including the Garrison) but it's probably more enjoyable to wander along at Scillonian pace or get a taxi to drop you off on one side of the island and walk back to your base. It's amazing what you come across on the coast path – the buckled steel plates of shipwrecks like the *SS Brodfield* on the rocks below the airport, a pillbox disguised as a wall at Old Town, Civil War batteries, a smuggler's cache in the cliff at Porth Mellon and the tombs of prehistoric Scillonians at Porth Hellick Down and Bant's Carn.

On the Garrison walls above Hugh Town.

HUGH TOWN, THE GARRISON, PORTHLOO AND PENINNIS

Hugh Town sits on a narrow neck of land below the headland called the Hugh (from the Cornish word *ughel* for *high place*), more commonly referred to as the Garrison. The town is the bustling hub of Scilly – most of the shops are here and all the off-island ferries leave from the quay, as does the *Scillonian*, signalling its arrival or departure with long blasts on its horn.

Three popular walks start from Hugh Town. Two are easy coastal walks, one to the rocky headland at Peninnis and the other along the more sheltered northern coast to Porthloo. But the first stop is a circuit of the Garrison walls. This is an excellent way to get your bearings as nearly all the off-islands can be seen as you walk around the headland. At Woolpack Point look south-west to Gugh, St Agnes and Annet with the Bishop Rock Lighthouse behind; at Steval Point, Samson comes into view followed by Bryher, Tresco and the western end of St Martin's. Don't worry if you struggle to tell them apart at first; until you get a mental map fixed in your head, they have a habit of appearing to blend into one another.

THE GARRISON, HUGH TOWN, PORTHCRESSA

The Garrison dominates the town with its almost continuous line of batteries, redans and walls. They were built in stages over about 400 years, starting with the Star Castle and ending with the early 20th century coastal gun batteries on the top of the headland. A whole circuit of the Garrison is about 2.4km (1½ miles).

A walk around the Garrison

The main access to the Garrison is up Garrison Hill from The Bank in Hugh Town (there's also access from Porthcressa through the Sally Port). Once at the gatehouse you can walk in either direction. Most people choose to turn south past Hugh House on the walls high above the town. The path gradually drops down to the water's edge, and at Morning Point you can walk outside the south-facing walls, a sunny place to stop and picnic. Now the views open up across to Gugh and St Agnes.

The beacon on Woolpack Rock and the Bartholomew Pole mark the width of the deep channel, St Mary's Sound. Listen out for the bell buoy marking the Spanish Ledges, the most southerly of the rocky hazards in St Mary's Sound. From Woolpack Point, a path turns inland and uphill to the 20th century gun emplacement of Woolpack Battery, a short cut past the campsite back to the Star Castle.

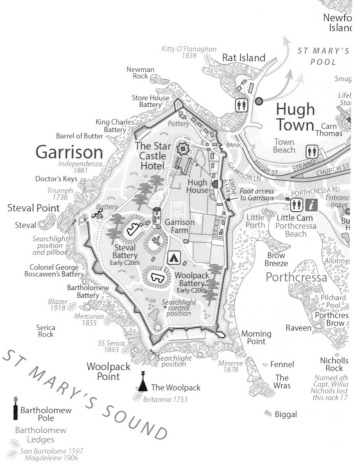

5

Looking over Porthcressa and Hugh Town from the path to Peninnis Head.

The coast path continues from Woolpack Point to George Boscawen's Battery. A narrow coast path does continue along the coast to Steval Point but most people turn inland at George Boscawen's Battery, following the rough track behind Lower Steval Battery as it heads uphill towards the Star Castle. If you want to join the coast again, a better-used path leaves this track about a hundred metres after the entrance to Steval and descends through the bracken to King Charles' Battery.

Hugh Town and Porthcressa

As we'll see later, from at least the 13th century Scilly's main settlement and harbour was at Old Town. The construction of the Star Castle in the 1590s shifted the island's centre of gravity to Hugh Town, and this then grew to become Scilly's major settlement. Its location on this narrow neck of land is a little precarious and there have been times within living memory when waves have washed right across it, flooding through the streets from Porthcressa to wash onto the back of Town Beach.

Porthcressa is St Mary's most popular beach, particularly for families with small children as cafes, loos and shops are all close-by. St Mary's other beach is at Pelistry on the east of the island in a more rural setting (but it has a cafe nearby too).

Buzza Tomb with Porthcressa and Hugh Town behind.

Buzza Hill and tower

Scilly's modest streams struggle to power a watermill and so this tower was built in 1821 to harness the wind (the base of another stands on the track to Peninnis Head). It's now open to the public as a camera obscura. A lens set at roof level projects the 360 degree view from the top of the tower onto a viewing surface below. It takes about forty-five minutes to complete a full rotation, picking out features like the lighthouses on the Bishop Rock (10.6km/6½ miles) and Round Island (7.4km/4½ miles). A prehistoric tomb stands nearby, the first of a number of Scillonian entrance graves we'll come across in this book.

The Garrison and Star Castle

In the medieval period, the rule of law on Scilly was administered from Ennor Castle at Old Town – Scilly's main settlement at the time. In practice, a blind eye was often turned to the activities of raiders and freebooters. At its mildest this could involve locals plundering any wreck that foundered on Scilly (even if that meant occasionally killing crew who made it ashore), but sometimes it involved pirates and privateers using Scilly as a base for harassing passing ships. The authorities on Scilly were not always strong enough, or willing enough, to oppose them, and anyway, as with the pillaging of the *Prinses Maria* on the Western Rocks in 1686 (see our St Agnes book), they could not always resist gorging on wrecks and their valuable cargoes if the opportunity arose. Mainly though, as long as any nefarious activity was confined to foreign ships, the government in London paid little heed, and anyway, until the reigns of Henry VIII and Elizabeth I there was really no permanent standing fleet to patrol the sea, which as a result was effectively a lawless realm.

That indifference changed in the late Tudor period as Scilly's strategic location next to the fast-growing trade routes to America and Africa brought it to the attention of national government. Its obvious

The Star Castle on the Garrison.

vulnerability to attack led to fears that it might be used as a base by a foreign power wanting to disrupt Britain's Atlantic sea trade. In order to address these concerns, the construction of a fort at Harry's Walls above Porth Mellon was started in 1550. However, the site was poorly chosen, and when tax revenues dried up during a downturn in the economy, it was abandoned unfinished.

The Spanish Armada of 1588 (despite its failure) again highlighted Scilly's acute vulnerability and renewed efforts were made to improve the island's defences. The focus shifted from Harry's Walls to fortifying the Hugh instead, and construction work on the Star Castle started in 1593 using the sort of geometric design favoured by Henry VIII (1491–1547) to construct castles on the south coast of England from Deal in Kent to Pendennis Castle at Falmouth.

The Garrison walls, intended to fortify the whole headland, were added in fits and starts, first, in the 1590s, across the neck above Hugh Town and then north to King Charles' Battery. There was a rapid acceleration in the mid 18th century as the struggles against Spain and then France flared up once more, and by the end of the 18th century all but a small stretch around Doctor's Keys was complete.

St Mary's Sound and Bartholomew Ledges

The broad expanse of St Mary's Sound is a little misleading as any ship coming into St Mary's Harbour has to follow a fairly narrow navigation channel close to the Garrison shore or risk being wrecked on the Spanish or Bartholomew ledges (the reefs are named after ships that foundered on them). These hazards make the sea between Bartholomew Pole and the coast of Gugh too dangerous for larger ships to navigate. The Cornwall and Isles of Scilly Maritime Archaeology Society have a great online virtual dive trail about the loss of the *San Bartolome* on the Bartholomew Ledges in 1597.

The gun platforms and batteries at Woolpack Point are sited at sea level so they could send their shot bouncing and skimming across the surface of the water to hit any ship at its most vulnerable point near the waterline. You'll also notice early 20th century defences here. A concrete searchlight position was intended to illuminate fast-moving hostile boats that might try to enter St Mary's Road at night. They could then be targeted by the quick-fire battery at Steval Point.

A path climbs up the hill behind Woolpack Point to one of two early 20th century coastal defence batteries on the Garrison (the other is not accessible to the public). They are part of a series of batteries built around the

The 20th century gun emplacement at Woolpack Battery.

British coast in the late 1890s when political instability and revolution in Europe revived fears of invasion. As the 19th century came to an end, Britain, France, Germany and Russia were engaged in an arms race, most obviously in the rivalry to develop ever larger and more powerful naval ships with guns that could fire many kilometres. The six-inch guns here were a better match for this threat. All these batteries were rendered obsolete, almost overnight, by the use of the first atomic bomb in 1945. English Heritage publish a book called *Defending Scilly* that details the evolution of the Garrison defences – it's available from the Paper Shop in Hugh Town.

Morning Point Battery on the Garrison (built 1742–43) looking over to Peninnis Head.

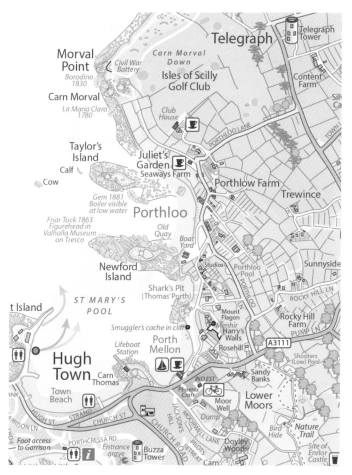

HARRY'S WALLS AND PORTHLOO

It's an easy 1.4km (¾ mile) walk from Hugh Town along sheltered coastline to Porthloo. Along the way you can take in the craft studios at the industrial estate behind Porth Mellon and, just before the beach at Shark's Pit (Thomas' Porth), you can climb up to the old fortifications at Harry's Walls. At Porthloo there are more craft studios to visit and it's just a short walk up to the cafe at Juliet's Garden where you can sit out overlooking St Mary's Road, or wander out to Carn Morval for a taste of wilder coastline.

If you would like a longer and different route back to Hugh Town, you can cross the island to Old Town (and Peninnis Head) by the Lower Moors Nature Trail. To do this from Porthloo follow Porthloo Lane to the junction with the main road at Rosehill. The gate in the hedge straight ahead of you is the start of Lower Moors Nature Trail. The trail weaves through reed beds, wetland and past pools to emerge on the coast at Old Town. From here you can follow the main road past the school and back to Hugh Town, but if you have time, the walk out to Peninnis Point is particularly beautiful in the early evening. From Peninnis either return along the coast path to Porthcressa or follow King Edward's Road back to Hugh Town. In all, a 5.3km (3⅓ mile) circular walk.

Harry's Walls above Porthloo. Mount Flagon Menhir, a prehistoric standing stone, stands right next to the cross-shaped shipping daymark.

Harry's Walls and Mount Flagon Menhir
Just after passing the lifeboat house at Carn Thomas, the road heads down to Porth Mellon. Leave the road at the back of the beach here and follow the sandy footpath to the rocks just before Shark's Pit (Thomas' Porth). A path leads up to Harry's Walls. Construction of a fort here started in 1550. New theories on gunnery angles and arcs of fire derived from the design of Italian Renaissance forts were used in the design. In this case the intended plan was for a square fort with a bastion on each corner. However, the location itself was not well chosen and gave only limited protection to shipping anchored in St Mary's Road. Two bastions and a connecting line of wall were all that was started, and construction was abandoned half finished when funding dried up in an economic downturn. It was decided that work to defend Scilly should start following the shock of the near invasion by the Spanish Armada in 1588. The focus shifted to fortifying the Garrison instead. A prehistoric menhir stands beside the shipping daymark.

Porthloo
Porthloo is a proper working cove. It's the main winter haul-out and maintenance base for sightseeing ferries. The island's gig club is also based here.

Shark's Pit (Thomas' Porth).

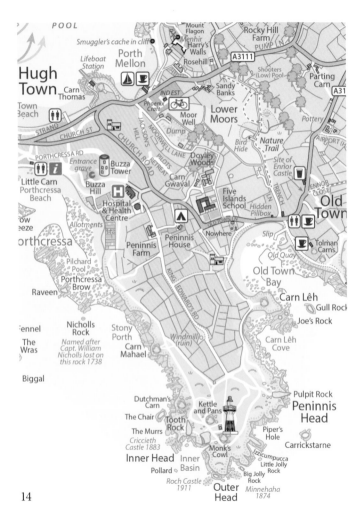

PENINNIS HEAD AND OLD TOWN

The walk from Porthcressa to Peninnis is a popular evening walk from Hugh Town. The rocky carns here are a first taste of the sort of granite landscape we'll encounter at Porth Hellick on St Mary's east coast, and on the off-islands. The easiest way to Peninnis from Porthcressa is to follow the coast path from the east end of the beach. It passes below Buzza Hill then turns inland for a short distance through the allotments before returning to follow the coast to Carn Mahael and Peninnis.

The shortest way to return to Hugh Town (if you don't return back along the coast) is to follow the high ground on King Edward's Road to Peninnis Farm and the Health Centre. From there, either keep straight on to Buzza Tower and down to Porthcressa or turn right at the Health Centre then left on Church Road. The distance from Porthcressa to Peninnis and back via King Edward's Road is about 3.2km (2 miles).

A longer walk crosses the island by the Lower Moors Nature Trail and Porthloo Lane (the Porthloo walk in reverse). Follow the coast path from Peninnis Lighthouse to Peninnis Head, the Pulpit Rock and Carn Lêh. The path joins the main road at Old Town (where there are cafes). Turn down Trench Lane by the side of Old Town

Inner Head at Peninnis looking over to the Spanish Ledges bell buoy and the southern tip of Gugh. Tooth Rock is in the foreground.

Cafe and follow the tarmac road for 100 metres. The road ends and it becomes a footpath. Follow the path and boardwalk through Lower Moors Marsh. You will eventually come out on the main road at Rosehill. Turn left for a quick return along the road to Hugh Town or follow the pretty lane straight ahead to Porthloo and Juliet's Garden Cafe where you can sit out on the terrace and enjoy the views with a drink. Then return to Hugh Town on the coast path to Shark's Pit and Porth Mellon. This longer walk from Porthcressa to Peninnis, Old Town, Lower Moors, Juliet's Garden, Porthloo and back to Hugh Town is about 6km (3¾ miles).

Peninnis Head and lighthouse

Peninnis is a dramatic place to visit at any time of day but it's particularly popular in the evening or when the sea is rough. Children love it for its exotic collection of odd-shaped – almost hallucinatory – rocks. Look out for the Monk's Cowl, the Toast Rack, Kettles and Pans, Pulpit Rock, the Tooth, the Turtle and the Claw. We'll come across many more named rocks like these such as the Loaded Camel at Porth Hellick, and the Nag's Head on St Agnes. Peninnis Lighthouse was erected in 1911 (1 white flash every 20 seconds) and formally superseded the old lighthouse on St Agnes.

The Kettles and Pans on Peninnis.

Old Town Harbour. Carn Lêh is in the middle distance and the Pulpit Rock on Peninnis Head is the flat horizontal rock silhouetted on the left.

Old Town and Ennor Castle

St Mary's was once connected by a land bridge from where Bar Point is today to Tresco and St Martin's. They in turn were connected by dunes and salt marshes to each other and to Bryher and Samson forming a single island, the Isle of Ennor. Old Town's ancient name was Porthennor – the harbour of Ennor – and it was from at least the 13th century the major settlement and landing place on Scilly. The island was administered from Ennor Castle. Little remains to be seen today apart from a few traces of walling (in a private garden), and the mound on which the castle sat (which even today forces the road to make a diversion around its base).

The old ruined quay that is revealed by the falling tide has its origins in the same period as the castle. Its curved arm and construction are similar to other early medieval quays in West Cornwall at Newlyn, Mousehole and Coverack. Although the harbour is now just a quiet backwater compared to the bustle of Hugh Town, a surprising amount of today's island life is centred here with the Five Island's School close by and many residents choosing to live here rather than in Hugh Town, which has a high proportion of holiday accommodation.

Old Town Church

If Ennor Castle was the seat of secular power on medieval Scilly then the priory church on Tresco, administered by monks from Tavistock Abbey, was the religious heart of the islands. It was they who established a church here sometime after AD1100. The original building has been rebuilt several times after falling into ruin. Until the 17th and 18th centuries when churches were built on St Agnes, Bryher and St Martin's, this church and the little chapels on Teän and St Helen's seemed to suffice for Scilly's needs.

The churchyard holds the graves of many shipwreck victims. It was usual until the 19th century for unidentified corpses and ordinary crew to be interred on the shore close to where they were found. There simply wasn't enough space to accommodate the dozens of victims that even a single wreck could bring, although exceptions were made for the high born and well-to-do. The officers who perished in the loss of the British Fleet in 1707 (see page 25) are buried here, as is the famous 18th century singer and actress Ann Cargill, who was drowned on the Western Rocks. The large obelisk marks a mass grave for victims from the *SS Schiller* (see our St Agnes book for more about all of them). Former prime minister Harold Wilson is also buried here.

Old Town Church.

Lower Moors Nature Trail

This trail, just like the Higher Moors Nature Trail at Porth Hellick, is a convenient short cut and a good way to make your own circular walks across St Mary's. It's mostly freshwater bog with reed beds, willow trees and beautiful yellow iris, which love the wet ground. The open fresh water attracts passing migrants, and there is a bird hide and boardwalk in the wetter areas. The start of the trail is at the end of Trench Lane that leaves the main road from beside the Old Town Cafe.

We'll continue along the coast to Porth Hellick, so walk along the track to Tolman Point and Porth Minick.

Peninnis Lighthouse with the Carrickstarne and Old Town Gilstone in the distance.

Porth Hellick.

OLD TOWN TO PORTH HELLICK AND HOLY VALE

The eastern side of St Mary's is the most varied and interesting part of the island's coastline, a lovely up-and-down mix of cliff and carn blended with sandy beaches and wide bays. It makes for happy exploring, from dodging landing aeroplanes at Church Point and sitting in a prehistoric cliff castle to seeking out the many tombs that sit on Porth Hellick Down. Combine that with the peacefulness of the sandy cove at Porth Hellick and the beauty of Pelistry and you have the ingredients for a good day out.

The bays at Old Town and Porth Hellick top and tail this short section of rugged and weather-beaten coastline. The wide bay at Porth Hellick is flanked on either side by carns and tombs. The beach at the head of the bay forms a natural barrier blocking the streams that fall from Holy Vale and Higher Moors to form Porth Hellick Pool, a popular spot for birdwatchers. The pool is the starting point for the Higher Moors Nature Trail, which meanders up the valley over boardwalks to the vineyards at Holy Vale.

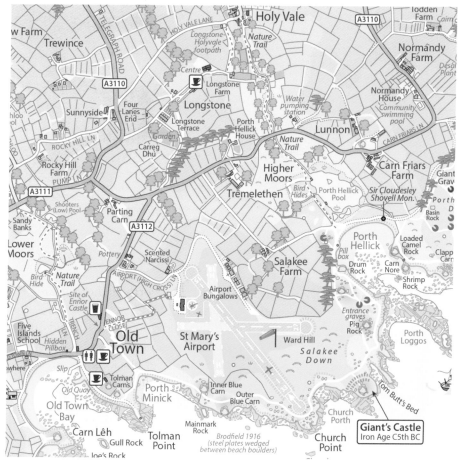

If you're over for a day trip from the mainland, this is an obvious area to explore as you can be on the coast path within minutes of landing at St Mary's Airport (take the footpath to Old Town in front of the terminal building). The walk from Old Town to Porth Hellick is about 2.4km (1½ miles). You can turn inland at Porth Hellick and return to Old Town or Hugh Town along the roads.

A circular walk from Hugh Town to Old Town, Porth Hellick, Higher Moors Trail and back along the road past Tremelethen to Porth Mellon and Hugh Town is about 5.3km (3¼ miles). If you extend your walk all the way to Holy Vale it's about 6.5km (4 miles) returning either along Holy Vale Lane or stopping in at Longstone Cafe for refreshments.

We'll start from Old Town and follow the coast to Porth Minick and Church Point.

Sea Kale at Porth Minick.

Porth Minick, Blue Carn and the *SS Brodfield*
Although Porth Minick is not the most picturesque of
Scillonian beaches, it does boast a most magnificent
collection of sea kale plants, the royalty of coastal plants.
For a vegetable whose domesticated relatives are usually
considered rather ordinary, its wild cousin is the most
beautiful and impressive of plants. From Porth Minick
the cliffs start to build in height. On the rocks below
Outer Blue Carn the rusting plates of the *SS Brodfield*
can be seen wedged between the rocks. She went aground
here in thick fog in November 1916 and, despite the
efforts of tugs, remained fast on the rocks and broke
apart in a gale a few days later.

Church Point, Giant's Castle and Tom Butt's Bed
It's called Church Point because fishermen use it and its
alignment with Old Town Church as a navigation mark
at sea. If a plane is coming into land, you will have to
wait before crossing the end of the runway here.

The Giant's Castle is a natural defensive site that
has been reinforced with four earth and stone banks.
The ramparts were probably surmounted with a timber
palisade. Similar ramparts occur on Shipman Head on
Bryher and (possibly) on Burnt Hill on St Martin's. Cliff
castles seem to date from around the 5th to 1st centuries
BC. They probably weren't permanent settlements as

Hull plates from the *SS Brodfield* on the rocks below Outer Blue Carn.

they're too exposed and rarely even have a water supply.
It's more likely they were built as temporary refuges
during periods of increased threat from sea raiders.

The name Porth Loggas possibly comes from the
Cornish words *lugh* for *calf* and *ogo* for *cave*, meaning
the cave of the calf – a seal calf presumably. Tom Butt's
Bed is named after a local lad who ran away from a cruel
master and took refuge in this cave. While his master
searched the downs, cursing and raging with a stick
to beat him, Tom was secretly supplied with food by a
kindly maid. He eventually smuggled himself onto a ship
at Hugh Town and sailed to the Southern Ocean.

Newfoundland Rocks claim the *Cita*

The *Cita* was on a tight schedule. She had called at
Rotterdam on 23rd March 1997 to pick up and offload
containers and, after a quick turnaround, headed to
Southampton. Following another swift turnaround
there she left for Ireland loaded with 112 containers.
As she steamed into the night, the captain and most of
the crew retired to bed and left the first mate in charge
of the bridge. He was tired and fell asleep, missing a
planned change of course that would have taken the
ship safely between Scilly and Land's End. Instead
at about 3.30am, with everyone fast asleep, the *Cita*
steamed straight onto Newfoundland Point.

The force of the impact punched a large hole in her
hull and she rapidly settled low in the water. It was soon
clear she would become a total loss. The ship gradually
listed over, shedding containers into the sea before
splitting in two, and slipping off the reef into deep
water. The containers that floated free drifted out to sea
where, in a repeat of the circumstance surrounding the
grounding of the *Minnehaha* in 1910 (see our Bryher
book), they were rounded up by local fishing boats and
landed as fair salvage from the sea.

Other containers ended up on local beaches where
old instincts were reawakened as islanders decided to

The trawler *Reginald* went aground on rocks near Porth Hellick Point
in 1902. Here the crew are making the best of the situation by having a
picnic while they wait for high tide.

liberate these 'gifts from the sea'. Scilly's constabulary
had to draft in officers from the mainland to watch over
the wreck day and night. In the past a wreck on Scilly
might have brought with it a huge haul of Spanish silver
coin, Aztec gold or exotic spices from the other side of
the world. In 1997 the treasures included toys, bathroom
accessories, golf bags, fork-lift trucks, polyester sheets,
toilet seats and garden gnomes – some of which you're
likely to come across as you walk past local gardens or in
your accommodation if you're staying on St Mary's.

Porth Hellick and Sir Cloudesley Shovell

This is one of St Mary's best places, a quiet beach and a good place to stop for a picnic and wade in the shallows. Judging from the concentration of monuments that flank the entrance to Porth Hellick and the small hill at the head of the bay, this was an important place for prehistoric Scillonians too, certainly for ritual and possibly as a landing place.

On the shore above the beach there is a small memorial to Admiral Sir Cloudesley Shovell (1650–1707). He was one of the most celebrated sailors of his time, a member of parliament and national heroic figure. At the age of fifteen, during the Second Anglo-Dutch War (1665–1667), he showed the sort of bravery that was later to become legendary by swimming between ships in the midst of action with battle orders in his mouth. He had a long and distinguished service, firstly in the struggle with the Dutch Empire and then against the French and pirates threatening Britain's trade routes in the Mediterranean.

In October 1707, Sir Cloudesley was returning from the Mediterranean with a fleet of twenty-one ships when they lost their bearings in bad weather and sailed right onto the Western Rocks. Three ships went down in quick succession. Sir Cloudesley's ship, *HMS Association*,

Sir Cloudesley Shovell (1650–1707).

25

struck the Outer Gilstone, *HMS Eagle* went down on Tearing Ledge close to the Bishop Rock and *HMS Romney* foundered on the Crebinicks. There was only a single survivor from these three ships, and more than 1,400 lives were lost, with bodies and wreckage washing up on Scilly and in West Cornwall for weeks.

The following morning Sir Cloudesley was washed ashore, barely alive, here at Porth Hellick. He was found next to the dead bodies of his two stepsons, their pet dog and another naval officer. Somehow they must have made it to a ship's boat or clung to wreckage because Porth Hellick is twelve kilometres from the Western Rocks. At that time it was lawful to remove objects from a corpse washed up on a beach but not to take things from the living who made it ashore. Sir Cloudesley was found by a local woman who, seeing a large emerald ring on his finger, is said to have suffocated him with her skirt.

As a temporary measure, he and the other victims were buried above the beach. A few days later his body was dug up, embalmed in a barrel of French brandy and transported to Westminster Abbey where he now lies beneath a grand memorial. His two stepsons, Sir John and James Narborough, are buried in Old Town Church. It's claimed that the emerald ring was recovered thirty years later when the woman who is supposed to have

Higher Moors Nature Trail.

murdered him confessed her crime on her deathbed. She gave the ring to a clergyman, who sent it to the Earl of Berkeley. He recognised it as the ring he had gifted to Shovell many years before.

Porth Hellick Pool

Porth Hellick Pool is a popular spot with birdwatchers because of the resident waders that live here and for the many migrant birds that stop off on their long journeys between southern Europe, Africa and the North. Scilly also gives hospitality to vagrant birds blown off course by Atlantic hurricanes (sometimes thousands of kilometres off course). They stop here for a few days to

Porth Hellick Pool.

rebuild their energy before setting off again. The pool is fed by one of the few freshwater streams on Scilly, and the boggy moors a little further up the valley provide a natural reservoir for much of the drinking water used on St Mary's. The water is extracted at the pump station by the road. In the high season, when demand outstrips the natural supply, water is also extracted from seawater at the desalination plant on Normandy Down.

Higher Moors Nature Trail and Holy Vale

The Higher Moors Nature Trail follows the side of Porth Hellick Pool, meandering through the reed beds (once used to supply withies for making crab and lobster pots) before crossing the road and continuing through the marshy elm woods to Holy Vale. The vineyards at Holy Vale have guided tours and there is a winery where you can taste the wines, but check opening times before you go. Holy Vale sits right in the centre of St Mary's so you can walk to almost any part of the island from here.

To return to Hugh Town, turn left along the stony track (Holy Vale Lane) to Rocky Hill Lane. To get to Longstone Cafe from Holy Vale, walk down Holy Vale Lane and, after sixty metres, a footpath (marked on the map as the Longstone–Holy Vale path) leaves on the left at Chy Mengleth.

The beach at Pelistry.

PORTH HELLICK DOWN, PELISTRY TO WATERMILL COVE

The cliffs and carns on the coast from Porth Hellick to Pelistry are backed by a plateau of heath several hundred metres wide. This zone is too exposed to be cultivated, and instead paths weave through the bracken, gorse and heather linking the granite carns with groups of prehistoric tombs, including the famous Giant's Grave. As well as searching out the tombs, it's also fun to locate the many striking and odd-shaped natural rocks that sit on the surface of the downs – the Basin, Pig, Horse and Drum rocks as well as the Druid's Chair and Bowl.

The heathland creates a buffer zone between the coast and flower fields, absorbing the force of the brute winds that buffet this coast in the winter. Further protection is provided by belts of planted trees and thick, close-set hedges. Set low down and almost out-of-sight between the hedges are neat rows of flowers. The crop is harvested in the winter months so the shelter is needed to shield them from strong winds which would flatten the crop in minutes. They are sent to the mainland to cheer up city dwellers with some Scilly colour.

At Normandy Down the coast turns towards the more sheltered waters of Crow Sound. The coast softens too as the Eastern Isles come into view, the heathland recedes and the fields, that up to now have been hiding at the back of the downs, reach all the way down to the shore. At Pelistry we'll find St Mary's best beach and at New Quay, a tiny slip so typical of Scilly – not much more than a channel cleared in the rocks.

The distance along the coast from Porth Hellick to Watermill Cove is 3.3km (2 miles). To make a circular walk, turn inland along Watermill Lane, Pungies Lane to Holy Vale and then down Higher Moors Nature Trail to Porth Hellick. A walk of 5.3km (3⅓ miles). There are refreshments along the way at Longstone and Carn Vean. It's a 2.4km (1½ mile) walk back to Hugh Town from Holy Vale along Holy Vale Lane.

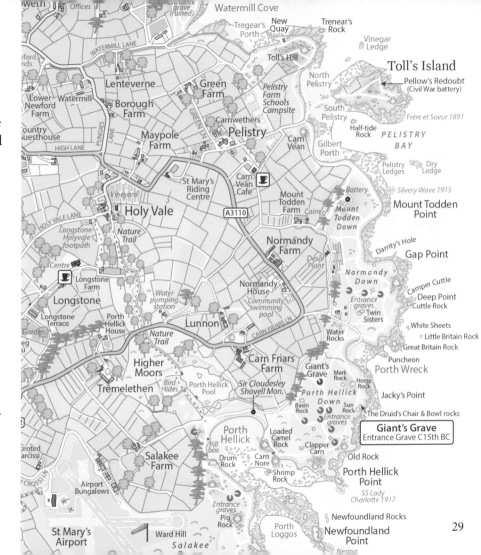

The Loaded Camel Rock (not showing its distinctive profile here) and Clapper Carn at Porth Hellick.

The Loaded Camel Rock.

Strange rocks of Porth Hellick

We've already seen some weird and wonderful rocks at Peninnis Head, and on the coast and downs around Porth Hellick there are more curious examples to look out for. The first is Drum Rock. It stands on the southern side of Porth Hellick and looks unusual not because of its size or shape but because it seems to have been turned on its axis, and now sits uncomfortably on the rocks below. This may have been a deliberate intervention by prehistoric Scillonians.

The area around Porth Hellick was obviously an important ritual place in prehistory (there are tombs on the hill close to the Drum Rock) and we know from similar ritual landscapes like Carn Galva in West Cornwall that there was a fashion for deliberately altering, realigning and manipulating great blocks in the Neolithic period (4000–2300BC). Sometimes that would mean turning them towards tombs or natural features in the landscape, presumably places with special meaning. Other large rocks were 'propped' by inserting smaller stones beneath them to form a window through which alignments could be viewed, or that capture significant moments like sunrise or sunset at a solstice (a rock inland of Dropnose Point on Gugh seems to be like this). These features are never conclusive, but the evidence seems to indicate these are probably deliberate, if subtle, human interventions.

Some of the natural rocks here manage to convincingly mimic organic forms (the Loaded Camel is the best known) and they too must have fired

Drum Rock.

The kerb of a tomb near Pig Rock at Porth Hellick. This is what a Scillonian tomb looks like in the 'wild' (compared to the Giant's Grave). Porth Hellick Down is in the distance with the Loaded Camel on the left and Clapper Carn on the right.

Basin Rock at the back of Porth Hellick Down.

Once exposed at the surface the wind and rain attack the joints and sculpt the rock into organic shapes – at least that is what we see when we look at them.

Another odd feature are the hollows and basins that form on the topmost surface of some rocks. The explanation is again straightforward: a shallow depression on top of the rock retains a pool of rainwater which, as it contains dissolved gases like carbon dioxide, is mildly corrosive. The water slowly dissolves the rock below and, over many centuries, the basins deepen and even become large enough for a child to bathe in.

However, the Victorians, with their fascination for all things to do with druids, liked to imagine the basins were carved to hold the blood of human sacrifices. The Druid's Chair on the cliff at Porth Hellick Down is said to be where the chief druid sat to watch the rising sun on the summer solstice. Nearby, set in the ground, is the Druid's Bowl where the human sacrifices were made.

The Druid's Chair.

the prehistoric imagination. Even modern humans, with our rational minds, are drawn to magical explanations and stories to explain their shapes. In fact, it's one of the pleasures of walking in granite landscapes that they offer so many opportunities for this sort of playful thinking. It's perhaps no surprise that prehistoric Scillonians chose this place, with its weird and magical rocks, as a home for their tombs and for the ashes of their ancestors.

We know, of course, that the cuboid shapes of the carns originate from when the granite, implanted deep underground as magma, cools, contracts and fractures (and not from giants assembling the carns by hand).

New Quay near Tregear's Porth.

Porth Hellick Down

Over the last 900 years Old Town churchyard has been the resting place for generations of Scillonians. Here on Porth Hellick Down you are standing in the Bronze Age (2300–700BC) equivalent. It's a ritual landscape thick with entrance grave tombs, some quite overgrown and some, like the Giant's Grave which are unusually large and very fine examples, having been excavated and partially reconstructed in the early 20th century.

Entrance graves (sometimes referred to as Scillonian passage graves or chambered tombs) are a type of Bronze Age tomb probably belonging to the first permanent settlers of Scilly. A low, stone-lined and roofed central passage or chamber is set inside a circular kerbed earth platform. They seem to have been constructed in the centuries around 2000 to 1500BC. The passage is just high enough to crouch in and is often a little wider in the middle. The entrance is sometimes closed off by small blocking or portal stones. Most chambers have been found empty, probably cleaned out in the past by treasure seekers and early archaeologists, but those that survived, usually because they collapsed long ago and were forgotten, seem to have held stacks of pottery urns holding the cremated remains of many generations along with collections of disarticulated bones.

The Giant's Tomb on Porth Hellick Down.

This type of tomb is rare in most of Britain, which seems to have belonged to a somewhat different tradition perhaps brought to Britain from Central Europe rather than from the Atlantic coast. A few examples do occur in West Cornwall (Ballowall Barrow near Cape Cornwall, Chapel Carn Brea, Treen Tombs near the Gurnard's Head), although they are far outnumbered by the more than seventy examples on Scilly. It seems this type of communal monument stayed in fashion for far longer here than on the mainland, where they were replaced by new tombs called cairns much sooner.

Tomb on Normandy Down.

Normandy Down and Mount Todden

There is a neat alignment of three entrance graves standing on Normandy Down. The very large white arrow next to them is a relict from World War Two. It was used by aircraft practising attack runs on a floating target anchored in Crow Sound. The point was to hone their skills for attacking U-boats found on the surface around the islands and in the Western Approaches.

Next we come to Mount Todden Battery – an odd hotchpotch construction, possibly a prehistoric tomb adapted to make a store for a Civil War battery, and then altered again for reuse in World War Two as a lookout.

Pelistry, Trenear's Rock and New Quay

This is St Mary's best beach. You can get here directly from Hugh Town by taxi or by walking along the road to Porth Mellon, turning left at Rosehill and then right along Rocky Hill Lane to Four Lanes and Holy Vale Lane and eventually Pelistry – a 3.5km (2¼ miles) walk. Time to stop for a swim or refreshments at Carn Vean Cafe. The coast path crosses the back of the beach towards Toll's Hill.

Shags and cormorants are almost always to been seen on Trenear's Rock where they stand with their wings outstretched, drying their feathers between diving for fish. Just around the corner is New Quay. On Scilly almost every isle has a 'quay' like this where boulders and rocks are cleared to one side to form a narrow channel just wide enough for a small fishing boat to land its haul of lobster and crab.

The path turns uphill and inland for a few hundred metres above Tregear's Porth before turning left along a track that runs between the fields to the beautiful inlet at Watermill Cove.

The *Scillonian* steams through Crow Sound on her way to Hugh Town. Cruther's Hill and Highertown on St Martin's are in the background.

INNISIDGEN, THE BAR, BANT'S CARN AND HALANGY DOWN

The northern end of St Mary's is a long way from the hubbub of Hugh Town and much closer to the more laid-back mood found on the off-islands. The coast, as it turns away from the open sea, mellows so that by the time you reach Bar Point the cliffs have melted away altogether and are replaced by banks of sand dunes. The Eastern Isles, which crept into view in the last section, now stand clearly across Crow Sound and as you round Bar Point, St Martin's, Tresco and the twin hills of Samson are also revealed.

This area was well populated in prehistory and we'll come across the remains of their fields, homes and tombs all along this coast. At that time a land link stretched north from Bar Point towards Craggyellis and Guther's Island, connecting St Mary's to Tobaccoman's Point on Tresco and Cruther's Hill on St Martin's. That old land surface was finally lost beneath the sea around the 10th century AD, but its approximate outline re-emerges on the lowest tides of the year when great areas of sand flats are exposed between the islands.

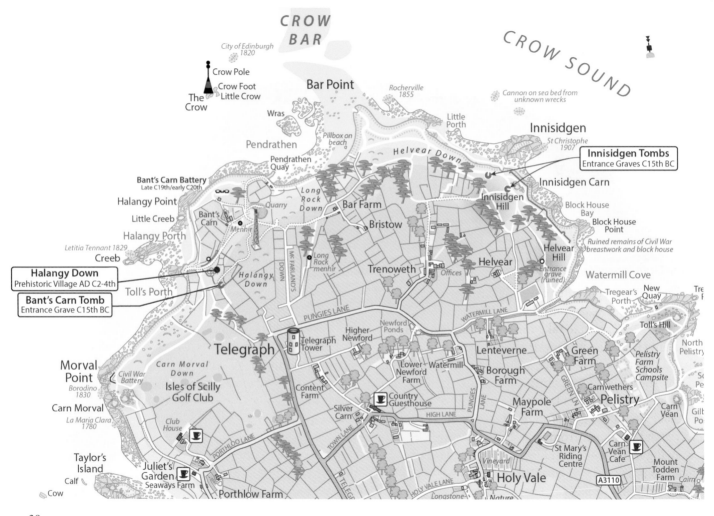

CROW BAR

CROW SOUND

City of Edinburgh 1820

Crow Pole
Crow Foot
Little Crow

The Crow

Bar Point

Rocherville 1855

Cannon on sea bed from unknown wrecks

Little Porth

Innisidgen

St Christophe 1907

Wras

Pillbox on beach

Helvear Down

Pendrathen

Pendrathen Quay

Innisidgen Tombs
Entrance Graves C15th BC

Innisidgen Carn

Bant's Carn Battery
Late 19th/early C20th

Halangy Point

Little Creeb

Halangy Porth

Letitia Tennant 1829

Creeb

Bant's Carn

Menhir

Long Rock Down

Quarry

Bar Farm

Bristow

Innisidgen Hill

Block House Bay

Block House Point

Ruined remains of Civil War breastwork and block house

McFARLAND'S DOWN

Long Rock menhir

Trenoweth

Offices

Helvear

Helvear Hill

Entrance grave (ruined)

Watermill Cove

Halangy Down
Prehistoric Village AD C2-4th

Bant's Carn Tomb
Entrance Grave C15th BC

Toll's Porth

Halangy Down

PUNGIES LANE

Higher Newford

Newford Ponds

WATERMILL LANE

Tregear's Porth

New Quay

Tre...

Toll's Hill

Morval Point

Borodino 1830

Carn Morval

La Maria Clara 1780

Civil War Battery

Carn Morval Down

Isles of Scilly Golf Club

Telegraph

Telegraph Tower

Content Farm

Lower Newford Farm

Watermill

Lenteverne

Borough Farm

Maypole Farm

Green Farm

Carnwethers

GREEN LANE

Pelistry Farm Schools Campsite

North Pelistry

So... Pe...

Pelistry

Carn Vean

Gilb... Po...

Club House

Silver Carn

Country Guesthouse

HIGH LANE

PUNGIES LANE

Taylor's Island

Calf

Cow

Juliet's Garden
Seaways Farm

PORTHLOO LANE

TOWN LANE

Porthlow Farm

TELEG...

Vineyard

HOLY VALE LANE

St Mary's Riding Centre

Holy Vale

Longstone

Nature...

A3110

Carn-Vean Cafe

Mount Todden Farm

Carn...

38

Bar Point with Tresco, Round Island and the western tip of St Martin's in the distance.

There is enough water covering Crow Bar (the sand bar that reaches north from Bar Point) on a normal high tide for the *Scillonian* to take this route on her way to and from Hugh Town Quay. If she left Penzance at the usual 9.15am departure time, she will steam into Crow Sound around 11.45am, coming in close to the shore at Innisidgen to avoid Hats Ledges (marked by the yellow and black buoy). It's great fun to sit on Innisidgen Carn and watch her appear from behind the Eastern Isles and swing into Crow Sound. For a ship that looks so big when you pass her berthed at the quay, she looks tiny set against the backdrop of the Eastern Isles. At low tide it's too shallow for the *Scillonian* to clear Crow Bar and then she is forced to take a longer course south of St Mary's and around the Garrison instead.

This 3.6km (2¼ mile) section of coast from Watermill Cove to Porthloo is easily walked in a morning or an afternoon. You can make it a 5.4km (3⅓ mile) circular walk by turning inland along the roads between Telegraph, Pungies Lane and Watermill Cove. Refreshments are at Juliet's Garden at Porthloo from where it's a 1.3km (¾ mile) walk back to Hugh Town.

We'll start from Watermill Cove, a beautiful narrow inlet and lovely place to swim when the tide is up.

Innisidgen Carn and tombs

There are two entrance graves at Innisidgen. The upper tomb, which stands right behind Innisidgen Carn is, along with the Giant's Grave and Bant's Carn, one of the best on Scilly. There's an information board at the site. The lower tomb is much less well preserved. It's likely that when they were constructed about 4,000 years ago, they sat above contemporary fields. This area was overwhelmed by drifting sand around the 1st century AD, and new fields and huts had to be rebuilt uphill and away from the rising tide of dune and sea. Those new fields were laid out around these tombs, which were ancient even then. The stepped terraces of the newer fields are most obvious around Lower Innisidgen Tomb.

Bar Point, Crow Bar and Pendrathen

The traces of prehistoric huts, field walls and even plough marks are preserved on the old soil surface under the dunes at Bar Point. There have long been tales of an old paved road that ran beneath the sand from Bar Point to Craggyellis and Guther's Island. No doubt a folk memory of a land bridge that did exist here until the early medieval period when it was lost to rising sea levels. In prehistory the view north was not sea but a mixed landscape of dunes, salt marsh and fields, perhaps with a few trees around Guther's Carn, similar to the landscape

The upper tomb at Innisidgen.

of Appletree Banks and Pentle Bay on Tresco today.

From Bar Point you now have a choice. The easiest option is to stick close to the shore following the coast to Pendrathen Quay and Halangy Down Ancient Village. Alternatively, take a diversion to see Long Rock standing stone, or menhir, at the back of Telegraph.

Long Rock menhir

To find this menhir walk to the back of the beach at Bar Point and take the well-used sandy track up through the trees towards the transmitter masts. A few metres past the entrance to Bristow and Bar Farm, a footpath heads off left among the pine trees to the back of the houses in Telegraph where you'll see the menhir. This is one of three good existing examples on Scilly; the other two are the Old Man of Gugh and the Mount Flagon menhir at Harry's Walls. They are usually thought to be among the oldest monuments in any landscape but, because they often stand in isolation, their exact age can be difficult to establish. However, flakes of Neolithic (4000–2300BC) flint were uncovered here in the 1920s.

Continue along the path to join the road at McFarland's Down. Turn left to see Telegraph Tower or right and down the track between the houses (keeping left where the track splits) to the sign for Bant's Carn Burial Chamber.

Long Rock menhir.

Telegraph Tower

This handsome tower was built in 1814 as an Admiralty signal station. Semaphore was used to signal to ships standing offshore. After Napoleon was defeated it was converted into a coastguard lookout. It's not open to the public. In 1869 a telegraph cable reached the islands from Nanjizal on the mainland. In 1898 that was superseded by a wireless station and then by the modern TV, radio and phone masts that stand here today. Return down the road at McFarland's Down to the sign to Bant's Carn Burial Chamber.

Bant's Carn Battery

The big six-inch guns in the Garrison batteries could deal with a threat from large battleships far out at sea, but there were concerns at the start of World War Two that St Mary's Harbour might be vulnerable to attack from small, fast-moving torpedo boats. This small battery, sited on the water's edge, was the response, although, by the time it was completed the threat had passed and it was never armed. It's one of a pair; the other is the smaller, lower battery at Steval on the Garrison. The building is private.

There is a path along the coast in front of the battery but it's little used and often overgrown and you will have to scramble down over the rocks and beach in places.

Most people just stay on the track that leads up from Pendrathen Quay (towards Telegraph) turning off after about 300 metres opposite the old quarry following the sign to Bant's Carn Burial Chamber.

Bant's Carn and Halangy Down Ancient Village

You might by now, after the tombs on Porth Hellick Down, Normandy Down and Innisidgen, be suffering from ancient tomb fatigue, but hold on for one last example, it's probably the best of all – Bant's Carn Tomb. Like other entrance graves, Bant's Carn Tomb was built in the Bronze Age about 4,000 years ago and, judging from the evidence of pottery fragments found inside, was in use for at least 500 years. Presumably, the fashion for burial or cremation changed after that or, perhaps, different structures like cairns took over as the preferred focus of prehistoric ritual. It has two very well-preserved kerbs and, just like the Giant's Grave on Porth Hellick Down, a small blocking or portal stone that restricts entry to the passage. Four cremations were found inside.

The original Bronze Age settlement, contemporary with the tomb, lay further down the hillside where Halangy Porth is now. The remains of hut walls, blackened fire hearths, discarded limpet shells (a staple food on Scilly from prehistory to the early 19th century) and pottery are slowly eroding out of the cliff there.

Early prehistoric fields here and at Bar Point as well as the first Bronze Age settlement seem to have been overwhelmed, not just by the sea, but also by drifting sand dunes in the Romano-British period 1,600 to 2,000 years ago. As a result, the village had to be relocated a little further uphill, and closer to Bant's Carn Tomb which, even then, was 2,000 years old. It's the remains of this later Romano-British village that are visible today and which you can wander around, walking in and out of their houses and along their streets just as they once did. There are information boards at the site.

Bant's Carn Tomb was originally sited on the rough, uncultivated ground above the first settlement, following the usual Scillonian pattern seen on Samson, Northwethel and Gugh. But as the village was forced to move up the side of the hill and away from the

Halangy Down Ancient Village.

Bant's Carn Tomb at Halangy Down Ancient Village. The rocks of the Creeb are in the middle distance with the twin hills of Samson behind.

advancing sand dunes, so the fields moved up with it. Traces of those fields are clearly visible all around the tomb as stepped terraces, which form over centuries as soil from ploughed fields is washed downhill to settle behind boundary walls. The same sort of stepped terraces surround Lower Innisidgen Tomb.

The new village included a courtyard house – a particularly West Cornish development of the Romano-British period (AD43–410). The excavated prehistoric villages at Chysauster and Carn Eûny near Penzance on the mainland are famous examples. A courtyard house incorporates the older, simple round hut design found everywhere on the islands (and under the sea) but adds small workrooms built against a thick enclosing wall forming a protected courtyard. There's a similar example at the prehistoric settlement on the shore of Nornour in the Eastern Isles.

To return to Porthloo you have the choice of keeping at a low level on the shoreline taking a path from near Bant's Carn Tomb or staying higher up the hillside. Both paths meet again at Carn Morval and join a track that passes through fields towards the road at Porthloo where it's time for a well-deserved crab sandwich and beer at Juliet's Garden.

Looking past Crow Pole to St Helen's and Round Island.

INFORMATION

Isles of Scilly Tourist Information Centre
Located above Porthcressa Beach on St Mary's.
www.visitislesofscilly.com
E: info@visitislesofscilly.com T: (01720) 620600

FERRIES AND SIGHTSEEING TRIPS

Ferries depart from Hugh Town Quay. Social media accounts and boards in Hugh Town give times and destinations for trips happening that day and are updated with the next day's trips in the early evening. Lots of choice; check out the boards on the quay. Buy your ticket at the kiosk on Hugh Town Quay or on-board.

St Mary's Boatmen's Association run most of the trips from St Mary's. Ferries run to the inhabited islands every day during the season with a rotating mix of wildlife and sightseeing trips to view seals, seabirds and the remote islands. A reduced service runs out of season and then you'll probably need to book.

Off-island ferries usually start leaving Hugh Town Quay at about 10.15am with returns throughout the day to late afternoon. Departure times and frequency change according to the tides, weather and time of year so check departure boards and social media accounts.

Buy your ticket at the kiosk on Hugh Town Quay, at the TIC and some hotels, or on-board.

BEST BEACHES

Porthcressa is popular with families as there are shops, cafes and loos right by the beach. Pelistry is more out of the way but is a very beautiful setting and Carn Vean Cafe is close by.

GETTING AROUND

The Scilly Cart Co

Hire 2, 4 and 6 seat electric carts for exploring St Mary's. Garage is situated on the Porthmellon Business Park.
www.scillycart.co
T: (01720) 422121 E: mail@scillycart.co

ACTIVITIES

Island Wildlife Tours

Naturalist Will Wagstaff leads half and full day walks around the islands plus regular slide shows in the Church Hall on St Mary's. Programme advertised on noticeboard at Hugh Town Quay and Tourist Information Centre.
www.islandwildlifetours.co.uk
T: (01720) 422212 E: will@islandwildlifetours.co.uk

Scilly Spirit Distillery, Old Town

Scilly Spirit produce award-winning Island Gin and Atlantic Strength Gin which is available to purchase online. They also have a Gin School where you can choose from a library of botanicals to make your own gin.
www.scillyspirit.com/shop
T: (01720) 422400
⊙ ✆ @scillyspirit f @scillyspiritdistillery

PLACES TO EAT

Check online or ring ahead as you may need to book in the summer months and in the quieter months some cafés don't open every day.

Carn Vean Cafe, Pelistry
Five minutes from Pelistry Beach. Open 10am to 5pm, closed on Fridays.
T: (01720) 423458 f @carnveancafe

Old Town Cafe

Longstone Lodge and Cafe
In the centre of the island, about 2km from Hugh Town. Good food, self-catering apartments, hostel accommodation and children's play area. Cafe open daily from 10am to 4.30pm. They also offer Friday night delivery service for a Scillonian Lobster meal.
www.longstonelodge.co.uk
E: longstonelodge@yahoo.com
f @longstonecafe ⊙ ✆ @longstonelodge

SHOPS AND GALLERIES

John Bourdeaux Pottery, Old Town
Open Monday to Friday, 10am to 1pm or by appointment. Visitors always welcome. Close to the Airport entrance.
www.johnbourdeaux.co.uk
T: (01720) 422025 E: bourdeauxpottery@gmail.com

CAMPSITE

Garrison Campsite and Holiday Cottages.
www.garrisonholidays.com
T: (01720) 422670 ✆ @garrisonhols

GETTING TO SCILLY

The Isles of Scilly are located 40km (25 miles) west of Land's End in Cornwall.

ARRIVING BY CAR

Head for Exeter then follow the A30 to Penzance. The A30 can be very busy on summer Saturdays and bank holiday weekends. To avoid the queues, aim to arrive on the Cornish border (about 1¼ hours from Penzance) before mid-morning or leave it until late afternoon/early evening. Flying from Exeter avoids Cornwall's congested trains and roads in the summer.

Parking in Penzance

You can't take your car to Scilly but there is secure parking at Land's End Airport, Penzance Heliport and in various locations around Penzance. Some secure parking sites are on the outskirts of Penzance so book parking when you buy your travel tickets and make sure you arrange a shuttle bus or taxi to take you to your departure point.

ARRIVING BY TRAIN

Penzance Station is served by direct trains from London Paddington and the North. The Night Riviera sleeper train leaves Paddington late evening and will get you to Penzance by about 8am the following morning. A shuttle bus runs between the station and Land's End Airport (12km/7½ miles) and Penzance Heliport. You will need to book a seat in advance and should aim to leave Penzance Station one hour before your scheduled take-off time. You can also get a taxi from the station forecourt. Passengers for the *Scillonian* can simply walk along the harbour to the Lighthouse Quay.

BY SEA ON THE SCILLONIAN

The *Scillonian III* sails to Scilly from around mid-March to the end of October. It usually departs Penzance at 9.15am with the return sailing leaving St Mary's at 4.30pm but departure times can vary depending on the tide and weather. The journey takes about 2¾ hours and you get a scenic view of the West Penwith coastline on the way.

In the busiest periods, there are two sailings a day, one departing Penzance at about 6am and one at 1pm. The return sailings from Scilly are at 9.30am and 4.30pm. Day trips to St Mary's from the mainland are possible if you leave on the early sailing. Many people book a late flight back on the Skybus to get the most time out of their day.

If you are staying overnight on Scilly, load your luggage into the container for your island at Penzance Harbour and attach a colour coded label to your bags. If you're staying on St Mary's you can have it delivered to your accommodation for a small fee (write where you're staying on your luggage label) or pick it up on the quayside when you arrive. Some accommodation providers will pick up you and your luggage by arrangement, otherwise you may need to book a taxi.

If you're staying on an off-island your luggage will be automatically transferred onto your off-island ferry at Hugh Town Quay and will be unloaded at your destination quay. Most accommodation providers will arrange to meet you at the quay to help you with your bags when you arrive. www.islesofscilly-travel.co.uk

BY SKYBUS

Skybus flies to Scilly all year round from Land's End Airport. You can also fly direct to St Mary's Airport from Newquay and Exeter airports; this is a more seasonal service. The flight from Land's End Airport takes about twenty minutes, from Newquay about thirty minutes and from Exeter about sixty minutes. A shuttle bus runs between the train station and Land's End Airport – you will need to book a seat in advance and should aim to leave Penzance Station an hour before your scheduled take-off time. You can also get a taxi from the station. www.islesofscilly-travel.co.uk

BY HELICOPTER FROM PENZANCE

There is a helicopter service from Penzance Heliport (near Sainsbury's as you come into Penzance on the A30) to St Mary's Airport and Tresco. The flight time from Penzance Heliport is about 15 minutes. On-site secure parking is available, as well as a shuttle from the train station. Bookings can be made on their website www.penzancehelicopters.co.uk or by calling T: (01736) 780828.

FERRIES AND SIGHTSEEING BOAT TRIPS

INTER-ISLAND FERRIES

Ferries run between the inhabited off-islands throughout the year. There's a reduced service out-of-season when you may need to book ahead. During the season (roughly end of March/Easter to the end of October) ferries usually start leaving at about 10.15am with returns throughout the day until late afternoon (subject to tide, weather and time of year). Buy your ticket at the kiosk on Hugh Town Quay or on-board. St Mary's Boatman's Association run most of the trips from St Mary's. If you're staying on an off-island, it will have its own boat service that runs daily services to St Mary's plus a rotating mix of circular and evening trips throughout the week. In addition to their main ferry, most have a smaller jet boat used for private charter and water taxi runs. Details of services are on social media and chalked on departure boards around the islands. Tresco, Bryher and St Martin's have more than one quay; your boatman will let you know where the return boat will pick you up.

SIGHTSEEING BOAT TRIPS

All island boat services offer circular sightseeing trips around the uninhabited islands during the season. With the exception of Samson, these don't land but afterwards you can usually land on the nearest inhabited off-island to stretch your legs, get a cup of tea and return on a later boat.

Samson

This is the only uninhabited island where ferries regularly land and it's a highlight of many holidays on Scilly. There are abandoned houses and prehistoric tombs to visit. Remember to take water, sun cream and a picnic with you as there are no cafés, shops or loos. Twin this trip with a visit to Bryher or Tresco.

St Mary's Circular

A circular trip around the whole island. A taste of the open sea and, if the tide permits, coming into some of the bays and inlets like Porth Hellick and Pelistry. A good choice for getting your bearings when you first arrive on Scilly as you'll pass all the other inhabited isles.
Trip takes 1¼ hours.

The Eastern Isles

This is probably the most popular sightseeing trip and the one with the calmest sea conditions. Great for watching and getting close to seabirds and Atlantic grey seals.
Trip takes 1¾ hours, also lands on St Martin's.

Annet, Western Rocks and the Bishop Rock Lighthouse

This boat trip is dependant on sea conditions being calm. If they're not, it might not run for a week or more, so if you have the opportunity, take it. If it's too rough to go all the way to the Bishop Rock Lighthouse, a shorter 1¼ hour trip runs to Annet for seals and seabirds.
Trip takes 2½ hours, also lands on St Agnes.

The Norrard (Northern) Rocks

A trip to the rocks and reefs to the west of Samson and Bryher – Illiswilgig, Scilly Rock and the Garden of the Maiden Bower. Look out for grey seals and puffins.
Trip takes 1½ hours, lands on Bryher/Tresco.

Holy Isles and Round Island Lighthouse

A trip around the small isles between Tresco and St Martin's – Round Island, St Helen's, Teän and Men-a-vaur.
Trip takes 1½ hours, also lands on Tresco, Bryher or St Martin's.

Follow the Gig Races

Follow the gig races from a sightseeing boat. Women race on Wednesday evenings and men on Friday evenings. The courses vary and trips often end up in an off-island pub.

Seabird Specials and Wildlife

Trips throughout the year to different parts of Scilly and the open sea. Includes evening trips to catch the return of shearwaters and puffins to Annet. Puffins are around from April to late July; shearwaters stay a few weeks later.

Ancient Scilly

Hear about the history and archaeology of Scilly with an expert on-board commentary as you cruise the islands.

Evening Supper Trips

A popular trip from St Mary's to the Turk's Head pub on St Agnes but other islands have similar specials too.